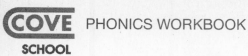

COVE SCHOOL — PHONICS WORKBOOK

Consonant
Blends & Digraphs

Part 2

Joyce Dadouche, M.A.
Laura L. Rogan, Ph.D.
Janis Wennberg, M.A.

Cove Foundation, Winnetka, Illinois

SRA/McGraw-Hill
Columbus, Ohio

ISBN 0-02-686974-8

3 4 5 6 7 8 9 10 MAL 99 98 97 96

Contents

clap

mitt

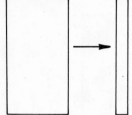

quack

wash

cuff

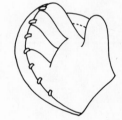

thin

frog

nest

flag

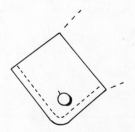

brush

 s ____ ell

 s ____ ip

 s ____ ip

 s ____ ap

 s ____ ab

 s ____ ick

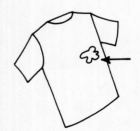 s ____ ot

 s ____ im

| n | c | p | w | l | m | k | t |

1. Chuck has a snack of _____ums and nuts.
   pl pr

2. Trish set the doll back in the _____ib.
   cr ch

3. The van will block the pa_____ when it stops.
   tt th

4. Ask Ed not to set his cup on the de_____.
   sh sk

5. Fill the gla_____ up to the top.
   ss sh

6. Mom will _____ess the red dress.
   pr pl

7. Tell Ann to _____op the nuts.
   cl ch

8. The ax is in the _____ed.
   sl sh

Compound Words

drum and stick is drumstick

check and up is checkup

up and hill is uphill

egg and shell is eggshell

catfish   is   _____   and   _____

      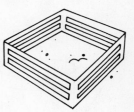

pigpen   is   _____   and   _____

nutshell   is   _____   and   _____

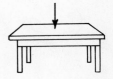

hilltop   is   _____   and   _____

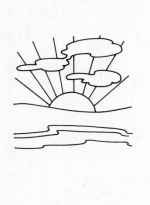

dustpan

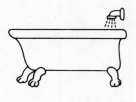

bathtub

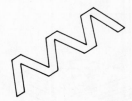

uphill

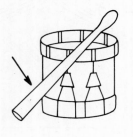

sunset

drumstick

zigzag

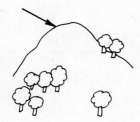

sunfish

dishpan

hilltop

snapshot

up - - - - - - - - - - - - - - - - to

in - - - - - - - - set

can   not

1. Pat did not cut the grass. Dad is __ __ __ __ __ .

_____

2. Fran __ __ __ __ __ __ swim past the dock.

_____

3. Drop the trash __ __ __ __ the trash can.

sun   tub

bob   cat

bath   set

4. Mom set the bath mat in the __ __ __ __ __ __ __ .

_____

5. The __ __ __ __ __ __ ran into the den.

_____

6. Beth will get to bed at __ __ __ __ __ __ .

he

she

me

we

Mom   will   be   glad.

me -

be

she

we

be

he

h ___

w ___

___ e

___ ___ e

___ e

___ e

sh ___

m ___

| h | m | sh | w | e | e | e | e | e |

14

be he she me we

---

1. Tom can skip well.

   _____ can skip well.

---

2. Beth will snap the lid on the can.

   _____ will snap the lid on the can.

---

3. We will be in class at 9:00.

   Miss Dunn will _____ with us.

---

4. Sam and I can plan a trip.

   _____ can plan a trip.

---

5. I will swim with Tad.

   Tad will swim with _____ .

| me | He | She | We | be |

1. Jill is not glad. _____ is upset.
   He She

2. Ron and I ran up the hill. _____ ran uphill.
   We Me

3. Ken has an egg. _____ will crack the eggshell.
   He Me

4. I can run to the bus stop.

   Al can run with _____.
   we me

5. We will _____ in the black van.
   be he

6. Dad and I got a cat.

   _____ got it from the pet shop.
   We Me

7. Ted has a sled. _____ has it on the hilltop.
   Be He

8. Pam has a dishpan.

   _____ will wash the dish in it.
   She He

___and

Jack and Jill

___ and

___and

___ ___ and

___and

___and

and	add	and	an	and	ask
land	land	lad	lab	lack	land
grand	grad	grand	gram	grand	grab
bland	black	band	bland	blot	bland
brand	brand	bran	Brad	brand	band
sand	sad	sap	sand	sack	sand

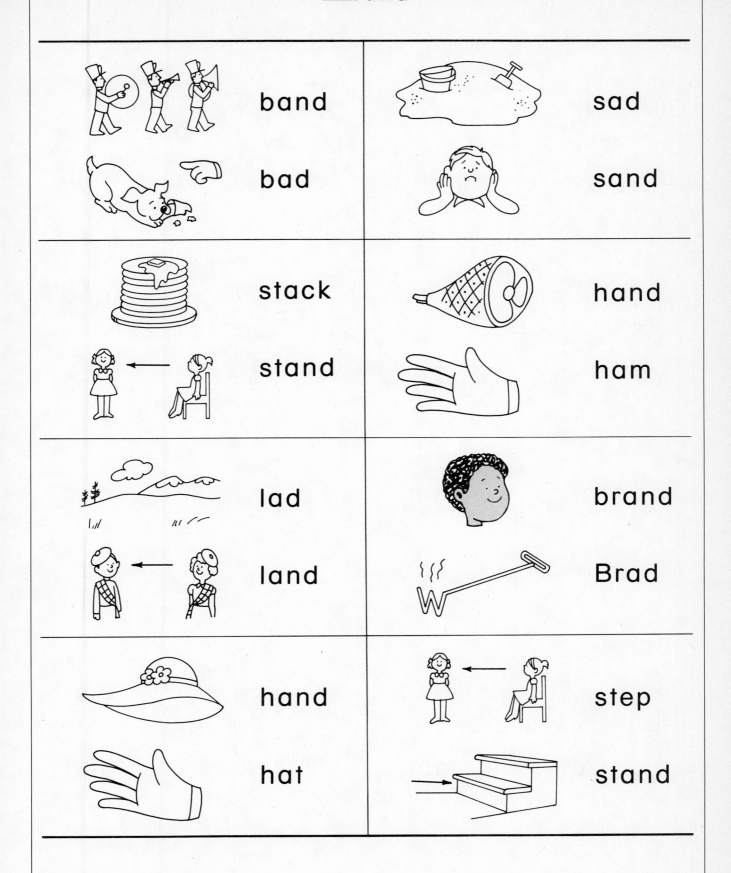

band

bad

sad

sand

stack

stand

hand

ham

lad

land

brand

Brad

hand

hat

step

stand

____ and

s ___
- ad
- and

b ___
- at
- and

b ___
- and
- ad

st ___
- and
- ack

h ___
- am
- and

s ___
- and
- ad

st ___
- and
- ack

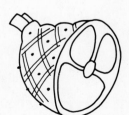
h ___
- am
- and

1. Which br_____ of hot dogs will be the best?
   and ag

2. Josh ran in the s_____ with his pet dog.
   and ad

3. Jill had to rush b_____ to class.
   and ack

4. H_____ the box of chips to me.
   and ad

5. He had to st_____ on the box to get the jug.
   and ack

6. Greg has the l_____ glass of pop.
   and ast

7. We will get off the jet when it l_____.
   ands ast

8. She will _____ if the small, red dress fits well.
   and ask

___end   ___ind   ___ond

___end

m___end

___end

___ind

___ond

___end

fond	fond	fund	hand	fish	fond
wind	win	wind	wins	wind	wick
spend	spell	send	spend	speck	spend
bond	bond	band	bond	back	bend
send	sand	send	sack	send	sick
lend	land	lend	led	tend	lend

| b | p | sp | w |

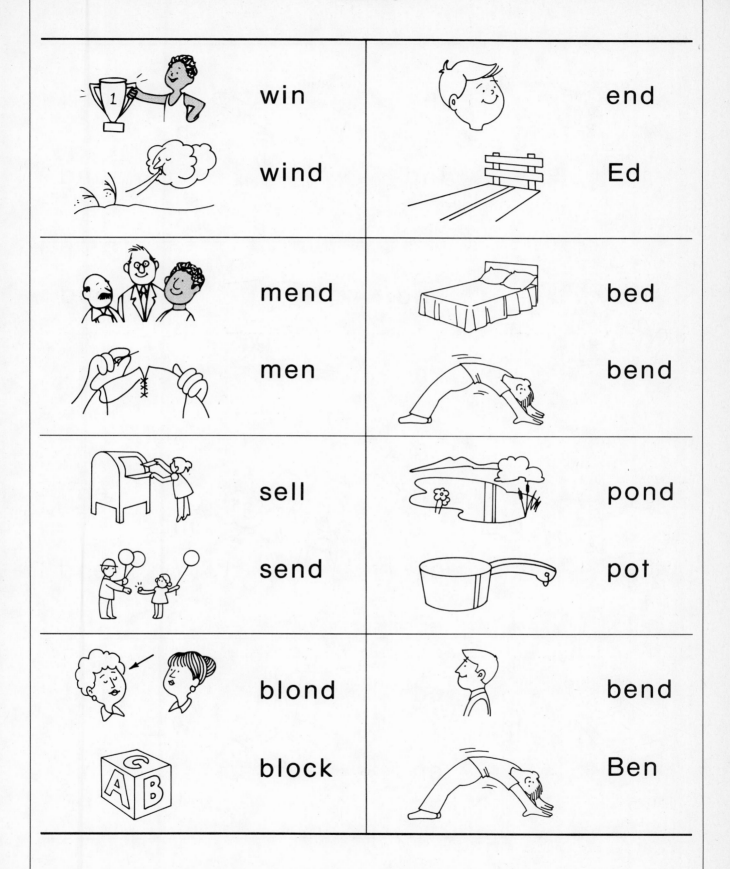

	win		end
	wind		Ed
	mend		bed
	men		bend
	sell		pond
	send		pot
	blond		bend
	block		Ben

w ___
in

ind

p ___
ot

ond

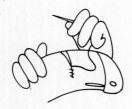

m ___
end

en

b ___
end

ed

p ___
ond

ot

m ___
en

end

b ___
ed

end

w ___
ind

in

1. Liz will m_____ the rip in the tan slacks.
   end   en

2. The frogs will be on the log in the p_____.
   ond   od

3. If Jeff runs fast, he will w_____.
   ind   in

4. Dad will l_____ his van to me.
   end   ed

5. Glen will not sp_____ all his cash.
   end   eck

6. Tom has a nap on his b_____.
   end   ed

7. The nest fell from the big gust of w_____.
   ind   in

8. The m_____ will stand at the bus stop with me.
   end   en

band

pond

mend

send

blond

bend

land

wind

sand

end

 bl___
ond
and
end

 s___
ond
and
end

 b___
ond
and
end

 w___
ind
and
end

 l___
ond
and
end

 p___
ond
and
end

 m___
ond
and
end

 s___
ond
and
end

1. Six men will be in the brass b_____ .
   and   ad

2. Max has f_____ when he digs in the sand.
   und   un

3. Fred is f_____ of his pal Liz.
   ond   ox

4. The red and black flag flaps in the w_____.
   ind   in

5. Did Miss Smith s_____ us the bill yet?
   end   ell

6. We will be gl_____ when Ann gets back.
   and   ad

7. Matt must not run past the e_____ of the block.
   nd   gg

8. Jan stacks the bl_____ in the box.
   onds   ocks

Not stop, but go .

Not yes, but no .

It is so hot.

The cab must stop, then it can _____ .
go no so

The dog will _____ up the hill with me.
no go so

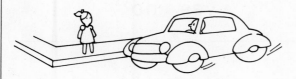

He will stop _____ that she can pass.
so no go

He has a bat. He has _____ bat.
go so no

go   stop

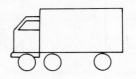

Is this a duck?
yes   no

Is this a top?
yes   no

go   stop

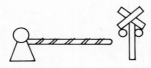

stop   go

Is this a frog?
yes   no

Is this a snack?
yes   no

stop   go

1. Can I run so fast that I will win?   yes   no

2. Can we get a desk from a pet shop? yes   no

3. Can the dog run uphill with me?   yes   no

4. Can a catfish swim?   yes   no

5. Will a fish swim into a pigpen?   yes   no

6. Can a trash can be on a sunset?   yes   no

7. Can a bath mat be in a bathtub?   yes   no

8. Can a sunfish go uphill?   yes   no

___ing

s ing

s t ing

___ing

___ing

___ ___ing

___ing

ding	dim	dig	ding	ping	ding
ping	ping	pin	ping	pig	ding
sting	sing	sting	stick	sting	sling
bring	big	brick	bring	brim	bring
sling	sling	sing	sting	slick	sling
thing	this	thing	thin	them	thing

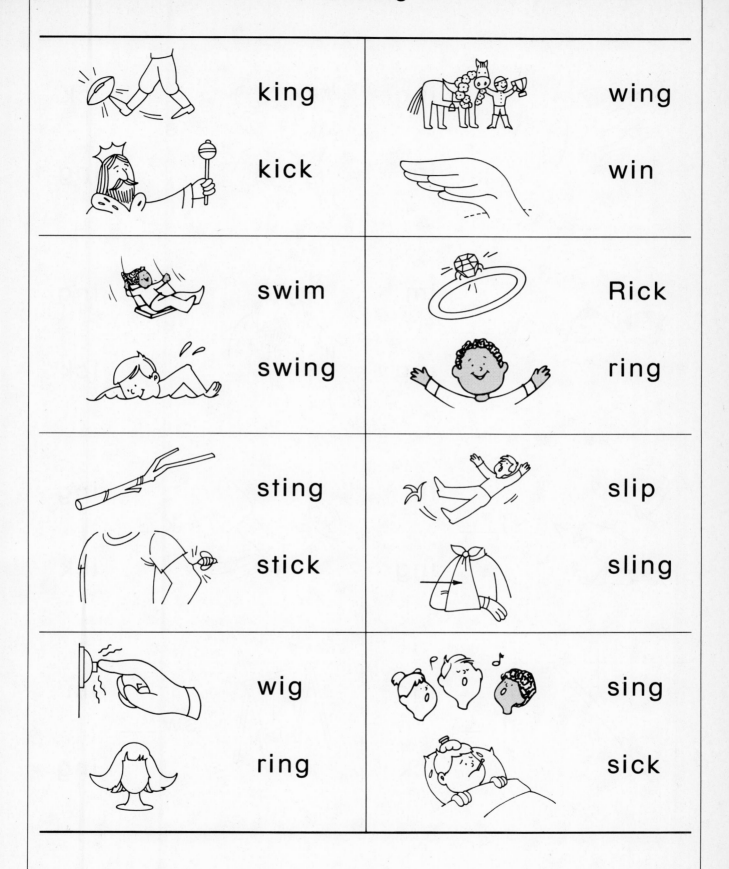

	king		wing
	kick		win
	swim		Rick
	swing		ring
	sting		slip
	stick		sling
	wig		sing
	ring		sick

___ing

w ___
ing
in

s ___
ick
ing

sw ___
im
ing

k ___
ing
ick

sl ___
ip
ing

k ___
ing
ick

st ___
ing
ick

sw ___
im
ing

1. Sal will br_____ a pad and pen to class.
   im   ing

2. The k_____ will go back to the bus.
   icks   ids

3. If he is hot, Dad will sl_____ off his vest.
   ip   ink

4. She has lots of th_____ in the chest.
   ins   ings

5. That bug in the net can st_____ him.
   ing   ill

6. We will go to the pond and sw_____.
   ing   im

7. Peg will r_____ the bell.
   ing   ich

8. The jet has big w_____.
   icks   ings

___ang   ___ong   ___ung

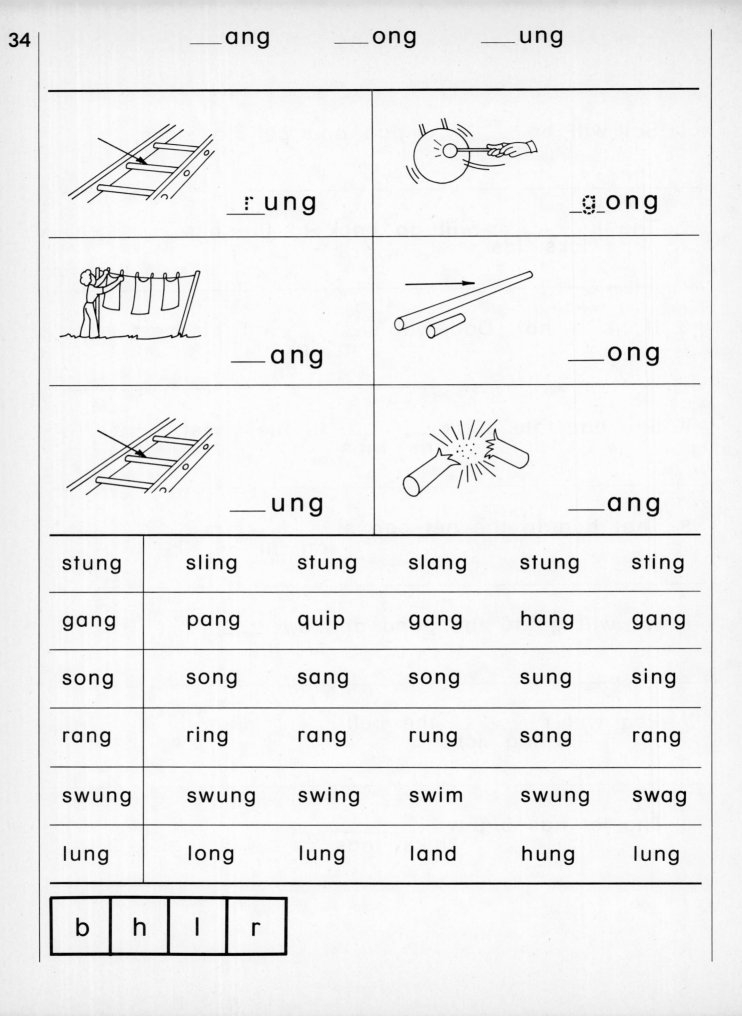

_r_ung	_g_ong
___ang	___ong
___ung	___ang

stung	sling	stung	slang	stung	sting
gang	pang	quip	gang	hang	gang
song	song	sang	song	sung	sing
rang	ring	rang	rung	sang	rang
swung	swung	swing	swim	swung	swag
lung	long	lung	land	hung	lung

b	h	l	r

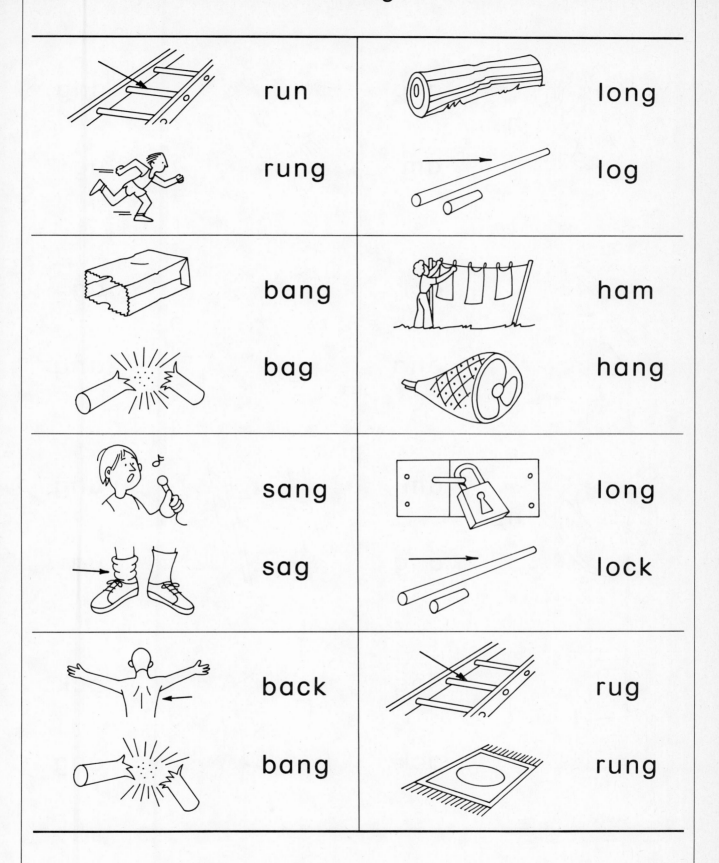

run

rung

long

log

bang

bag

ham

hang

sang

sag

long

lock

back

bang

rug

rung

___ng

h___

ang

am

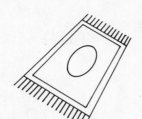
r___

ung

ug

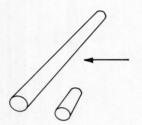
l___

ock

ong

b___

ag

ang

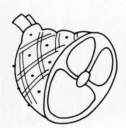
h___

am

ang

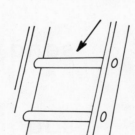
r___

ung

un

l___

ong

ock

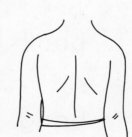
b___

ack

ang

1. Beth h_____ up the wash in the sun.
   ung   ug

2. Pam will go on a l_____ trip with me.
   ong   og

3. Vann will fill the b_____ with gumdrops.
   ag   ang

4. The truck is st_____ in the sand.
   ung   uck

5. We will h_____ up the swing.
   ash   ang

6. The bug st_____ Deb on the leg.
   ack   ung

7. Brett will toss his s_____ into the wash.
   ongs   ocks

8. The g_____ will rush to get on the bus.
   ang   ag

swing

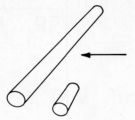

long

ring

hang

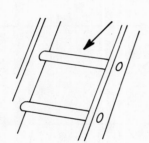

king

rung

sting

gang

sing

sling

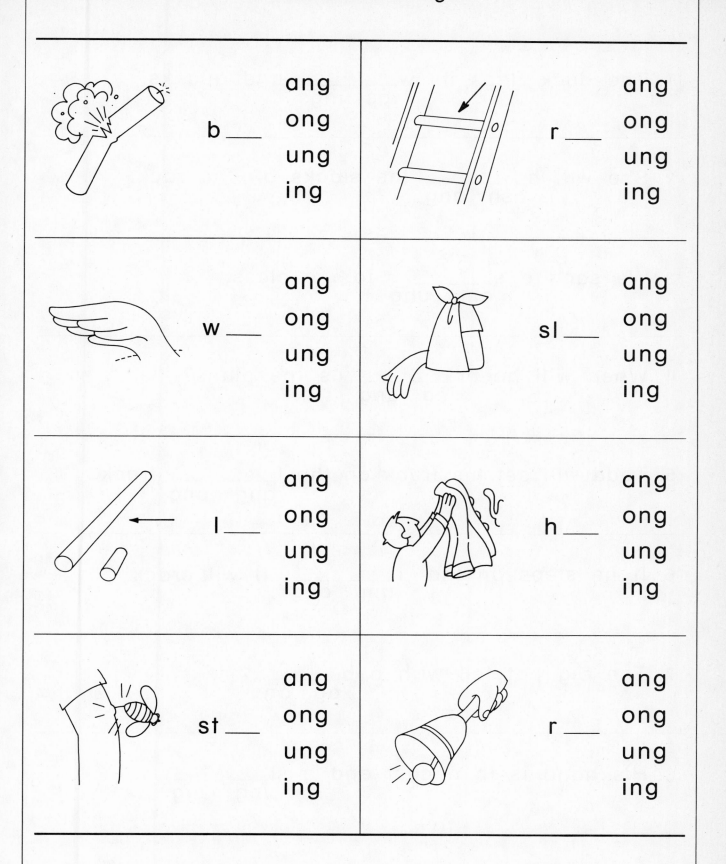

b ___   ang
         ong
         ung
         ing

r ___   ang
         ong
         ung
         ing

w ___   ang
         ong
         ung
         ing

sl ___   ang
         ong
         ung
         ing

l ___   ang
         ong
         ung
         ing

h ___   ang
         ong
         ung
         ing

st ___   ang
         ong
         ung
         ing

r ___   ang
         ong
         ung
         ing

1. The duck flaps its w_____ and quacks.
   igs   ings

2. She will h_____ the slacks on the rack.
   ash   ang

3. We sang a s_____ to the class.
   ong   ung

4. When will he br_____ us the plans?
   ing   ung

5. Todd will set his truck on the l_____ track.
   ang   ong

6. If he steps on that r_____, it will crack.
   ung   ang

7. The big pot fell with a b_____.
   ag   ang

8. His hand is in a cast and a sl_____.
   ing   ung

swing

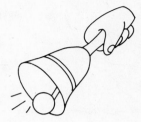

end

gang

stand

rung

ring

blond

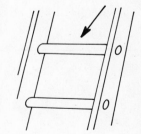

send

king

bend

___nd ___ng

l___	und ung and ang
r___	end ing und ung
g___	and ang ond ong
s___	end eng ind ing
r___	and ang und ung
l___	and ang ond ong
bl___	ond ong end eng
s___	ind ing and ang

 w _____

 h_____

 s_____

 b_____

 h_____

 w_____

 b_____

 s_____

| and | and | and | ind | ang | ang | ing | ing |

1. Did the w_____ bend the stem?
   ing ind

2. Mom will bl_____ the mix in the pan.
   end ess

3. Dad will go and get a box of small _____.
   ends eggs

4. Will he run with me to the sw_____?
   ings ims

5. Pam had on the bl_____ wig.
   ond ock

6. The bug st_____ me on the leg.
   ung uff

7. Mom will h_____ up the wash.
   and ang

8. I w_____ that I had a sandbox.
   ing ish

The clock can tick.

The clock is ticking.

The cab can back up.

The cab is back_____ up.

Mom will dust the top of the desk.

Mom is dust_____ the top of the desk.

The dog can sniff at the pup.

The dog is sniff_____ at the pup.

The chick can peck at its shell.

The chick is peck_____ at its shell.

She can ring the bell.

She is ring_____ the bell.

Miss Smith will stand in back of me.

Miss Smith is stand_____ in back of me.

Ken can hang up his slacks on the rack.

Ken is hang_____ his slacks on the rack.

1. He is _____ to the swing set.
   run running

2. The dog will _____ so he can get a snack.
   beg begging

3. The pup is _____ in the sandbox.
   nap napping

4. Vic is _____ to get slim.
   jog jogging

5. Jack can _____ the ball to Bill.
   batting bat

6. Mom is _____ up the handbag.
   zipping zip

7. The tall man can _____ the big dog.
   pet petting

8. The pup is _____ at the rag.
   tug tugging

push

pull

put

me   you

1. Scott will pu___ ___ me.

2. Jim will pu___ ___ the duck.

3. If you sit in the sun, ___ou will get a tan.

4. Mom will pu___ the box on the desk.

pu __ __

pu __ __

__ ou

pu __

pu __

pu __ __

pu __ __

__ ou

sh	sh	ll	ll	t	t	y	y
pull	push	put	you

1. Todd will _____ his sled up the hill.
   pull   put

2. Did _____ swim in the big pond?
   yet   you

3. He _____ the pup on the grass.
   put   push

4. Jill will _____ the dish on the stack.
   push   put

5. Did _____ quit the job?
   you   yet

6. Ann will _____ the stick into the hot dog.
   push   pull

7. Did she press the slacks _____?
   yet   you

8. Jill will _____ the tag off the dress.
   push   pull

	__b elt		__w ilt
	__ __ilt		__elt
	__ilt		__ilt

pelt	pet	pelt	pelt	pest	belt
tilt	till	kilt	tilt	lit	tilt
felt	felt	fell	felt	fed	belt
wilt	will	wilt	wit	wilt	with
kilt	kilt	kit	tilt	kick	kilt
melt	met	men	melt	melt	mill

k	m	qu	t

	bell		wilt
	belt		Will
	kilt		belt
	kit		bed
	stilt		men
	stick		melt
	quill		felt
	quilt		fell

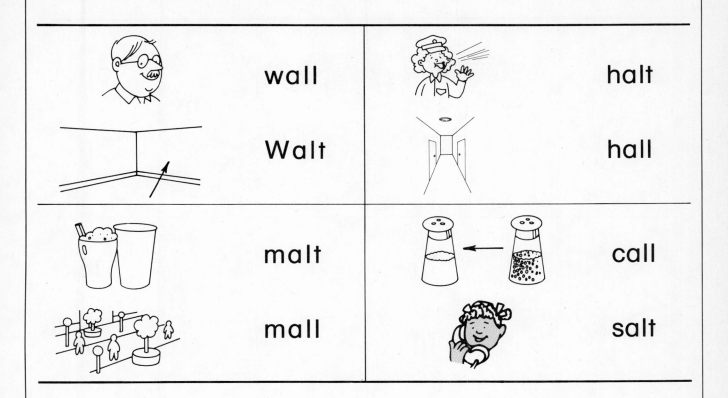

	wall		halt
	Walt		hall
	malt		call
	mall		salt

1. Meg and I will go to the shopping _____ .
   malt   mall

2. Roz is hanging a snapshot on the _____ .
   Walt   wall

3. We will get a _____ at the snack shop.
   malt   mall

4. Tell Brad not to add much _____ to the eggs.
   salt   call

5. We put a big clock on the wall in the _____ .
   halt   hall

s___

and

alt

m___

all

alt

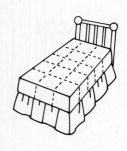

qu___

ilt

ill

st___

ick

ilt

h___

alt

all

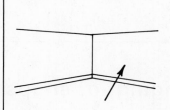

w___

all

alt

k___

it

ilt

qu___

ilt

ill

1. Which b_____ will go with the black slacks?
   ell elt

2. We can go swimming if it is st_____ hot.
   ilt ill

3. If she puts that in the sun, it will m_____.
   et   elt

4. Matt f_____ sick so he had to rest.
   elt   elf

5. The dog will sm_____ the cat.
   ell elt

6. Mom is putting the qu_____ at the end of the bed.
   it ilt

7. Fred is putting s_____ on his eggs.
   ack alt

8. The pot f_____ off the sill.
   elt ell

56

__elf __olf __elk __ilk

	elf
	elk
__ilk	
	__elf
__olf	
	__ __elf

sulk	sulk	silk	sell	sulk	self
milk	mill	milk	mitt	mist	milk
bulk	bulk	hulk	bulk	buck	back
silk	sick	sulk	silk	silk	sill
golf	gulf	golf	gill	golf	gull
self	send	sell	self	fell	self

g	m	s	sh

	sill		shell
	silk		shelf
	golf		elf
	gull		egg
	milk		sick
	mill		silk
	sell		elk
	self		end

1. The cat will lick up the m_____ in the dish.
   ill   ilk

2. Did you put the salt back on the sh_____?
   elf   ell

3. Miss Grand will lend us six e_____ .
   lks   ggs

4. Mom has a pink and black s_____ dress.
   ill   ilk

5. Deb is picking up sh_____ from the sand.
   elfs   ells

6. Meg is running to get the lost g_____ ball.
   olf   ot

7. Jack cannot pick up the box hims_____.
   ell   elf

8. Walt will s_____ if he cannot go with us.
   ung   ulk

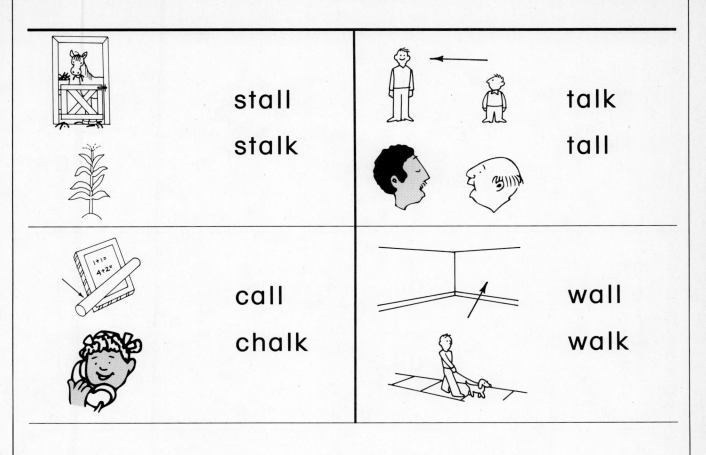

stall
stalk

talk
tall

call
chalk

wall
walk

1. Kim can _____ the dog to the pond.
     wall walk

2. Walt has a box of _____ on the desk.
                      chalk call

3. That windmill is big and _____ .
                            talk tall

4. He will wash the _____ in back of the bathtub.
                     wall walk

5. The van did _____ , but Mom got it to go.
                stalk stall

   m___   ilk
                        ill

   s___   ell
                        elf

   w___   all
                        alk

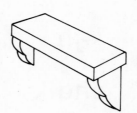   sh___   elf
                        ell

   t___   alk
                        all

   s___   ill
                        ilk

    s___   ell
                        elf

   sh___   elf
                        ell

 chal___

 mel___

 gol___

 el___

 stal___

 mil___

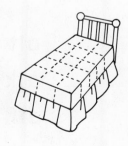 quil___

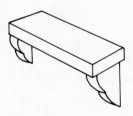 shel___

| k | k | k | f | f | f | t | t |

___ lt   ___ lf   ___ lk

b ___
elt
elk
elf

e ___
lt
lk
lf

s ___
ilt
ilk
ilf

m ___
alt
alk
alf

t ___
alt
alk
alf

st ___
alt
alk*
alf

g ___
olt
olk
olf

s ___
alt
alk
alf

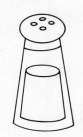

chalk

malt

shelf

elk

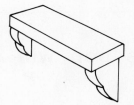

salt

golf

milk

elf

walk

wilt

1. Walt will t_____ to his pal from class.
   all alk

2. The cab will st_____ if it has no gas.
   alk all

3. The plant will w_____ if it is put in the hot sun.
   ill ilt

4. Miss Smith will let Chuck get the ch_____.
   ap alk

5. The pop will spill if you t_____ the glass.
   ilt ing

6. Dad will get g_____ clubs from the shop.
   olf ong

7. When w_____ we go shopping?
   ill ilt

8. Jeff will get a m_____ with his snack.
   all alt

_h_ elp

_g_ ulp

___eld

___eld

___elp

___elp

weld	well	weld	wed	held	weld
gulp	gulp	gull	golf	gulp	gulf
help	hull	hill	help	held	help
held	help	held	halt	held	weld
yelp	yell	yelp	yet	yes	yelp
kelp	held	help	kelp	yelp	kelp

h	h	w	y

1. Think of a wish at the wishing w_____ .
   eld ell

2. I h_____ the glass when Pat put milk in it.
   en eld

3. His mom is fond of g_____ .
   olf ot

4. The man in the pet shop will s_____ me a fish.
   ell elf

5. Dad will tell Fred not to g_____ his malt.
   ull ulp

6. Resting in bed will h_____ Jan get well.
   elp em

7. The pup will y_____ if he gets himself stuck.
   et elp

8. Mom will h_____ the slacks.
   elp em

wilt

stilt

elf

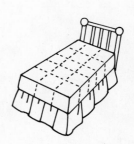

chalk

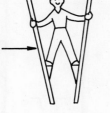

help

golf

elk

quilt

weld

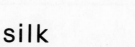

silk

sh___	elf elt elp eld
s___	alf alt alp ald
b___	elf elt elp elk
w___	ilf ilt ilp ilk
w___	alf alt alp alk
m___	alf alk alt ald
m___	ilf ilk ilp ilt
y___	elf elk eld elp

1. Bess will w_____ with us to the bus stop.
   alt alk

2. Sal will go shopping and get a s_____ dress.
   ill ilk

3. The pond will m_____ in the spring.
   elt eld

4. Roz is st_____ putting the cans on the shelf.
   ilt ill

5. I h_____ the pup when it got a checkup.
   eld elp

6. If Rick t_____ his glass, it will spill.
   ills ilts

7. She will h_____ him wash his dog.
   eld elp

8. I w_____ ask Peg to push me in the swing.
   ilt ill

___ink

<u>ink</u>	<u>:</u> ink
___ink	___ ___ink
___ ___ink	___ink

link	land	link	lick	luck	link
blink	blink	bland	black	blink	blond
rink	mink	rink	rich	rink	nick
brink	brand	brick	brink	brim	brink
clink	clink	link	clack	click	clink
mink	mink	rink	mink	nick	sink

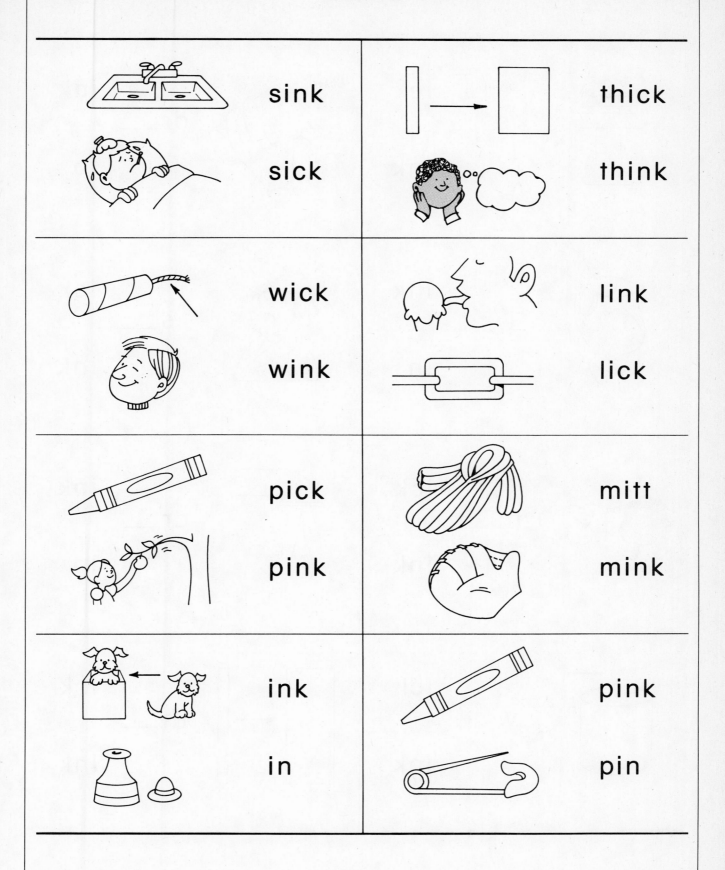

sink

sick

thick

think

wick

wink

link

lick

pick

pink

mitt

mink

ink

in

pink

pin

s ___
  ick
  ink

dr ___
  ink
  ip

w ___
  ink
  in

s ___
  ick
  ink

th ___
  ick
  ink

dr ___
  ink
  ip

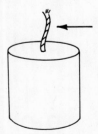

w ___
  ick
  ink

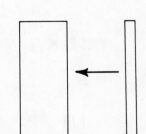

th ___
  ick
  ink

1. We will walk to the r_____ with them.
   ink ich

2. Ask Jan to grab the end of the st_____.
   ink ick

3. Deb is filling the glass at the s_____.
   ick ink

4. The stem has a p_____ bud on it.
   ink ick

5. The dog l_____ me on the hand.
   ink icks

6. Beth th_____ a trip on a jet is so grand.
   inks ins

7. She is getting the ball and running w_____ it.
   ink ith

8. Jeff has a dr_____ of milk with his snack.
   ip ink

__ank __onk __unk

h_ onk

t_ h_ ank

__ank

__ __unk

__unk

__ank

crank	rank	crank	crack	crash	crank
dunk	duck	bunk	dunk	bank	dunk
honk	bank	honk	hock	tank	honk
rank	rank	rack	rank	ran	rink
chunk	chick	chunk	chum	chunk	chuck
plank	plank	plunk	plan	lack	plank

b	b	sk	t

back	drink
bank	drill
bunk	sack
bun	sank
trunk	tan
truck	thank
hog	track
honk	trunk

 th ___   an

    ank

 b ___   un

    unk

 h ___   onk

    og

 b ___   ank

    ack

 b ___   unk

    uck

 h ___   og

    onk

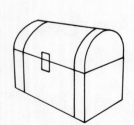 tr ___   uck

    unk

 d ___   unk

    uck

1. He will th_____ Mom when she gets back.
   ank   an

2. She has to go to the b_____ to cash a check.
   ank   unk

3. The small pup has lots of sp_____.
   ank   unk

4. We dr_____ from the big mugs.
   ank   unk

5. His job will be to help fix the pl_____.
   anks   unks

6. The cab h_____ so the bus will stop.
   unks   onks

7. He is tossing the tin cans in with the j_____.
   unk   ust

8. Walt has a b_____ bed with a red quilt.
   ank   unk

trunk

honk

thank

pink

tank

link

ink

junk

drink

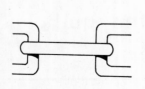

bunk

 tr ___ ink / ank / unk / onk

 st ___ ink / ank / unk / onk

 t ___ ink / ank / unk / onk

 w ___ ink / ank / unk / onk

 h ___ ink / ank / unk / onk

 r ___ ink / ank / unk / onk

 sk ___ ink / ank / unk / onk

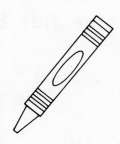 p ___ ink / ank / unk / onk

1. Mom is talking to the man at the b_____.
   ank   unk

2. He is pressing the lid on the can of dr_____ mix.
   ink   ank

3. The d_____ is quacking and snapping at a bug.
   unk   uck

4. When will the club pl_____ a trip to a pet shop?
   an   ank

5. Liz has to get rid of the j_____ in the shed.
   ust   unk

6. I th_____ that I will go and get a checkup.
   ank   ink

7. Will you put the flat box on top of the tr_____?
   unk   ust

8. He will h_____ so he will not get in a crash.
   onk   ank

drink

trunk

stand

pond

bend

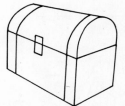

skunk

end

think

band

thank

___ nd   ___ nk

t ___

and
ank
end
enk

w ___

ond
onk
ind
ink

h ___

ond
onk
and
ank

b ___

and
ank
und
unk

m ___

und
unk
end
ink

st ___

end
enk
and
ank

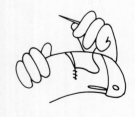

m ___

end
enk
und
unk

p ___

und
unk
ond
onk

 p_____

 w_____

 p_____

 j_____

 sk_____

 b_____

 bl_____

 b_____

| end | ind | ond | ond | ank | ink | unk | unk |

1. Meg will sp_____ cash on a hot dog and malt.
   end   ed

2. Beth must step up to get to the top b_____.
   uck   unk

3. The big chest fell off the ship and s_____.
   ank   and

4. If she b_____ the stick, it will snap.
   ends   eds

5. Tell Skip to go wash up at the s_____.
   ick   ink

6. We toss rocks into the p_____.
   ond   od

7. Sal rests in the s_____ and gets a suntan.
   ank   and

8. Dad is filling in the bl_____ on the check.
   ands   anks

   bank

                                    sing

   wink

                                    honk

   bang

                                    sink

   hang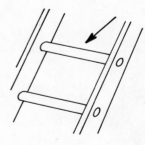

                                    long

   swing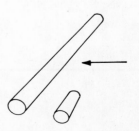

                                    rung

h ___
- ank
- ang
- onk
- ong

r ___
- ink
- ing
- ank
- ang

sl ___
- unk
- ung
- ink
- ing

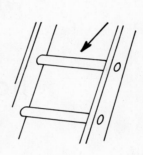

r ___
- ank
- ang
- unk
- ung

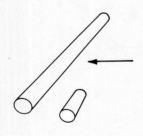

l ___
- onk
- ong
- unk
- ung

sk ___
- ink
- ing
- unk
- ung

h ___
- ink
- ing
- onk
- ong

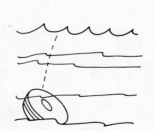

s ___
- ank
- ang
- onk
- ong

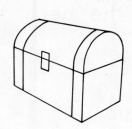 tr_____

 r_____

 b_____

 st_____

 h_____

 r_____

 st_____

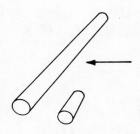 l_____

ink | ink | onk | unk | ang | ing | ing | ong

1. Fran is putting the p_____ quilt on the bed.
   ink   ing

2. His small ship s_____ in the bathtub.
   ang   ank

3. H_____ had to push his van when it got a flat.
   ang   ank

4. I h_____ on to the end of the stick the pup had.
   ung   unk

5. The dog is smelling the tracks of the sk_____.
   unk   ull

6. Will you help h_____ the slacks on the rack?
   ank   ang

7. Spot will br_____ the stick back to me.
   ing   ink

8. We will b_____ on the drums in the band.
   ank   ang

tank

pond

mend

gang

ring

bend

long

rink

junk

sand

___nd   ___ng   ___nk

	sink		hand
	sing		hang
	wing		bank
	wink		band
	sand		stink
	sank		sting
	rink		wink
	ring		wind

bl ___
ond
ong
onk

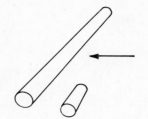
l ___
ond
ong
onk

st ___
ind
ing
ink

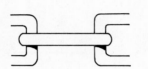
l ___
ind
ing
ink

sl ___
ind
ing
ink

l ___
and
ang
ank

tr ___
und
ung
unk

s ___
end
eng
enk

___end ___ond ___ang ___ing ___ung ___ank ___ink

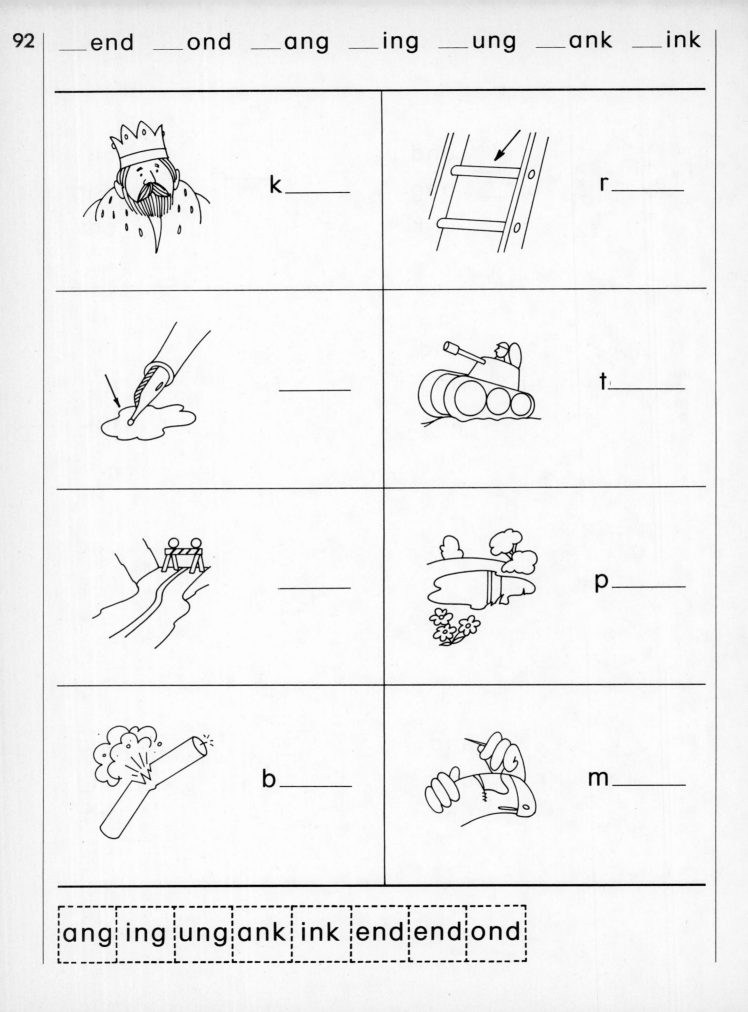

k_____

r_____

_____

t_____

_____

p_____

b_____

m_____

ang | ing | ung | ank | ink | end | end | ond

1. When the bell r_____, we must hand in the quiz.
   ings inks

2. If you sp_____ all the cash, you cannot get a ball.
   end ed

3. H_____ gets no cash if the grass is not cut.
   ang ank

4. The pup got a whiff of the sk_____ and ran.
   unk ull

5. The jet will l_____ so that we can get off.
   and ad

6. She will thank me if I help br_____ in the wash.
   ink ing

7. Fran is putting the snapshots into the tr_____.
   unk ust

8. The g_____ is glad to let you walk with them.
   ag ang

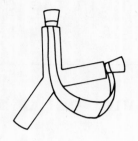

bathtub

slingshot

handbag

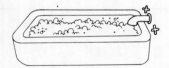

sandbox

handstand

windmill

milkman

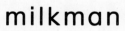

shellfish

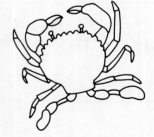

spl

str

spr

shr

thr

squ

scr

tw

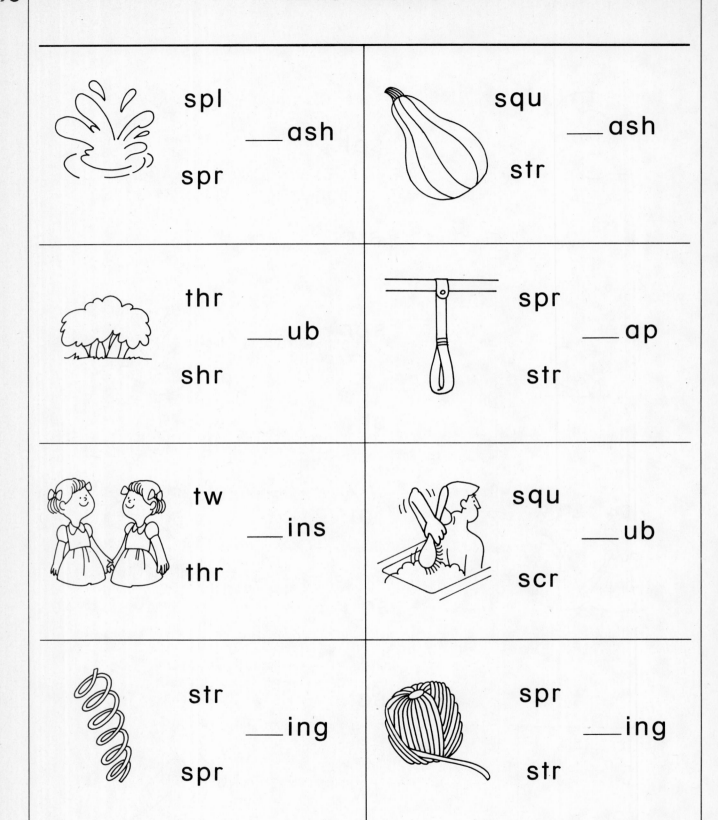

spl
spr   ___ash

squ
str   ___ash

thr
shr   ___ub

spr
str   ___ap

tw
thr   ___ins

squ
scr   ___ub

str
spr   ___ing

spr
str   ___ing

 sc_____ub

 sp_____ing

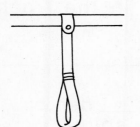 st_____ap

 sh_____ug

 sp_____ash

 st_____ing

 s_____ash

 t _____ig

| r | r | r | r | r | w | l | qu |

1. Mom will _____ub the spot off the silk dress.
            st   scr

2. The skunk is running into the _____ed.
                                     shr   sh

3. Bill will _____ash the box and put it in the trash.
            squ   scr

4. When the pup gets a bath, he will _____ash.
                                    st   spl

5. His cap _____ank when Mom put it in the wash.
            shr   sh

6. He _____uck the list up with a tack.
      st   str

7. Dad pulls a _____ig off and sticks a hot dog on it.
              st   tw

8. In the _____ing we can go fishing.
          spr   s

___ent

99

d__ent

t__ent

___ent

___ent

___ent

___ent

tent	ten	tent	test	tell	tent
rent	rent	red	rest	rent	runt
went	wet	went	west	went	when
spent	speck	sent	spent	sped	spent
lent	lent	let	lent	lens	lint
Kent	Ken	Kent	king	kick	Kent

b	s	sp	K

© 1995 SRA/McGraw-Hill

___ nt

	spent		brick
	speck		Brent
	Ben		tent
	bent		ten
	desk		lent
	dent		leg
	bent		deck
	bed		dent

 r ___
ed
ent

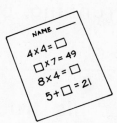 t ___
ent
est

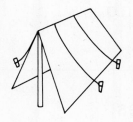 t ___
ent
est

 sp ___
ed
ent

 s ___
et
ent

 w ___
ent
et

 b ___
est
ent

 r ___
est
ent

1. The cub is running back into his d_____.
      en   ent

2. Hank l_____ his truck to his pal.
     et   ent

3. She held up the r_____ and black flag.
        ed   ent

4. We will put up a t_____ on the grass.
         ent   en

5. Frank w_____ with Josh to get a malt.
        est   ent

6. Mom sp_____ a lot of cash at the shopping mall.
       ent   eck

7. Dad went and got us t_____ cans of pop.
           ent   en

8. Fran s_____ a check to the bank.
       ent   et

ant	_s_ _q_ _u_ int
__ants	__ __int
__ __ant	__int

lint	lint	list	lint	lens	led
stunt	stunt	stunt	stun	stuff	stun
squint	squish	squint	squid	squash	squint
front	from	front	frost	front	frog
splint	splint	split	plant	splint	slit
print	print	prim	pin	rent	print

m	p	pl	pr

squint

squid

mint

mitt

ax

ant

pans

pants

hunt

hut

splash

splint

pin

print

pant

Pat

h ___
it

int

h ___
unt

ut

p ___
ants

ans

pl ___
an

ant

squ ___
id

int

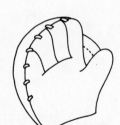
m ___
int

itt

a ___
x

nt

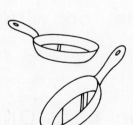
p ___
ants

ans

1. Fred put the m_____ in a small dish.
   ints itts

2. The dog will p_____ if he is in the hot sun.
   at ant

3. Pat is getting a hot dog on a b_____ at a stand.
   un unt

4. The man will pl_____ grass in front of the shed.
   an ant

5. The spr_____ in the bed is sticking up.
   ing int

6. Pam squ_____ when she is in the sun.
   ints ids

7. He struck the log with his ax and spl_____ it.
   int it

8. Jim is asking Miss Ott to help him pr_____.
   im int

print

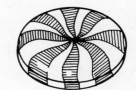

dent

ant

squint

hunt

tent

plant

sent

pants

mint

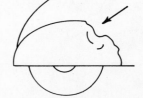

Review ___ nt

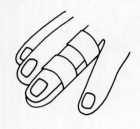 spl___
- int
- ant
- ent
- unt

 pl___
- int
- ant
- ent
- unt

 sp___
- int
- ant
- ent
- unt

 s___
- int
- ant
- ent
- unt

 h___
- int
- ant
- ent
- unt

 p___
- ont
- ant
- ent
- unt

 pr___
- int
- ant
- ent
- unt

 m___
- int
- ant
- ent
- unt

1. Roz will pr_____ with chalk.
   im int

2. The bug is stuck in the w_____.
   ent eb

3. The van has a d_____ in it.
   en ent

4. Put the cl_____ on the desk.
   ips ints

5. Mom will pl_____ shrubs in the fall.
   ank ant

6. The vet will put a spl_____ on the dog.
   it int

7. The stalk of the tall plant is b_____.
   en ent

8. The pup is pulling the rag fr_____ his hands.
   om ont

__anch   __ench   __inch   __unch

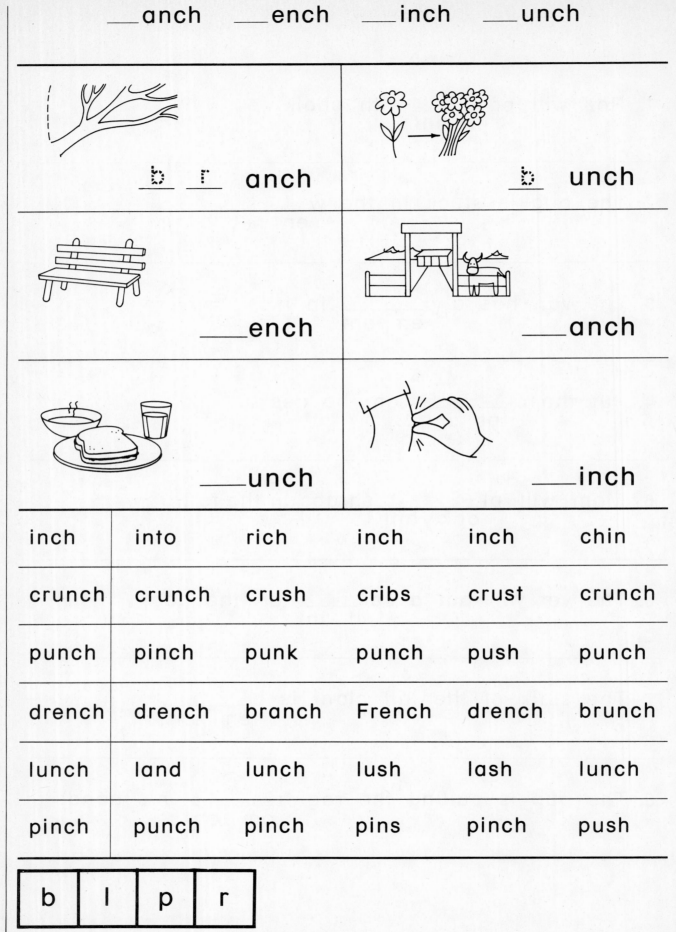

b r anch

b unch

__ench

__anch

__unch

__inch

inch	into	rich	inch	inch	chin
crunch	crunch	crush	cribs	crust	crunch
punch	pinch	punk	punch	push	punch
drench	drench	branch	French	drench	brunch
lunch	land	lunch	lush	lash	lunch
pinch	punch	pinch	pins	pinch	push

| b | l | p | r |

ranch	pinch
ran	pin
in	Ben
inch	bench
bun	branch
bunch	band
lunch	pump
luck	punch

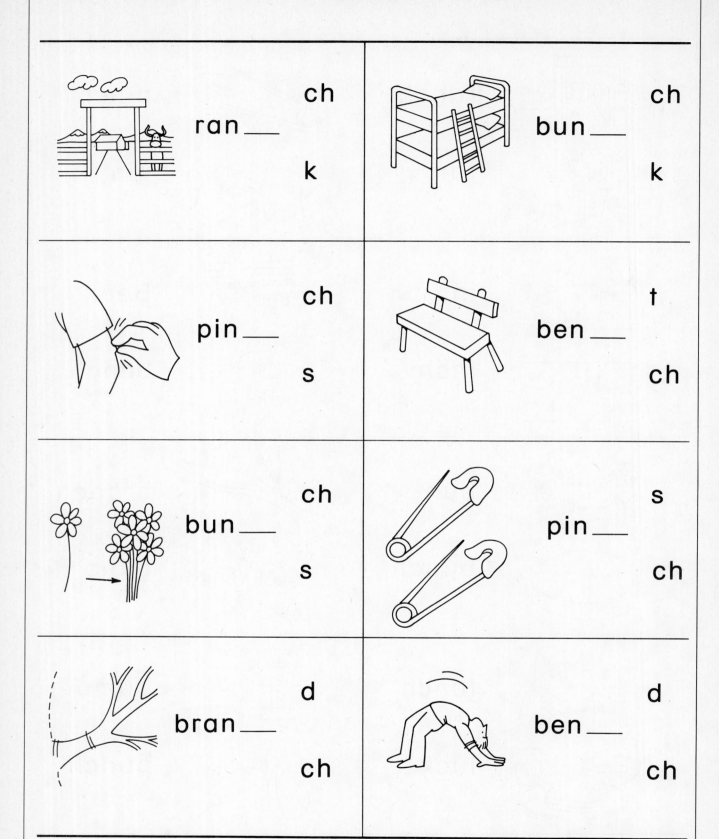

ran___   ch   k

bun___   ch   k

pin___   ch   s

ben___   t   ch

bun___   ch   s

pin___   s   ch

bran___   d   ch

ben___   d   ch

1. Mom and Dad will stop and rest on the ben____.
   t   ch

2. The bran____ fell from the strong wind.
   ch   d

3. The P_____-Pong ball went into the net.
   ing   inch

4. Dad will add a pin____ of salt to the mix.
   s   ch

5. Jill will mun____ on the chips in the dish.
   k   ch

6. Which bran____ of milk did you get?
   ch   d

7. The bobcat is stalking the hens on the ran____.
   t   ch

8. Liz is asking Mom to hem the dress an in____.
   to   ch

_atch

l atch	s c r atch
__ atch	__ atch
__ atch	__ atch

batch	bash	batch	latch	bath	batch
scratch	scratch	scram	snatch	scratch	catch
latch	lash	batch	latch	last	latch
snatch	scratch	snatch	smash	snatch	match
patch	patch	path	patch	push	past
match	math	match	mash	much	match

c	h	m	p

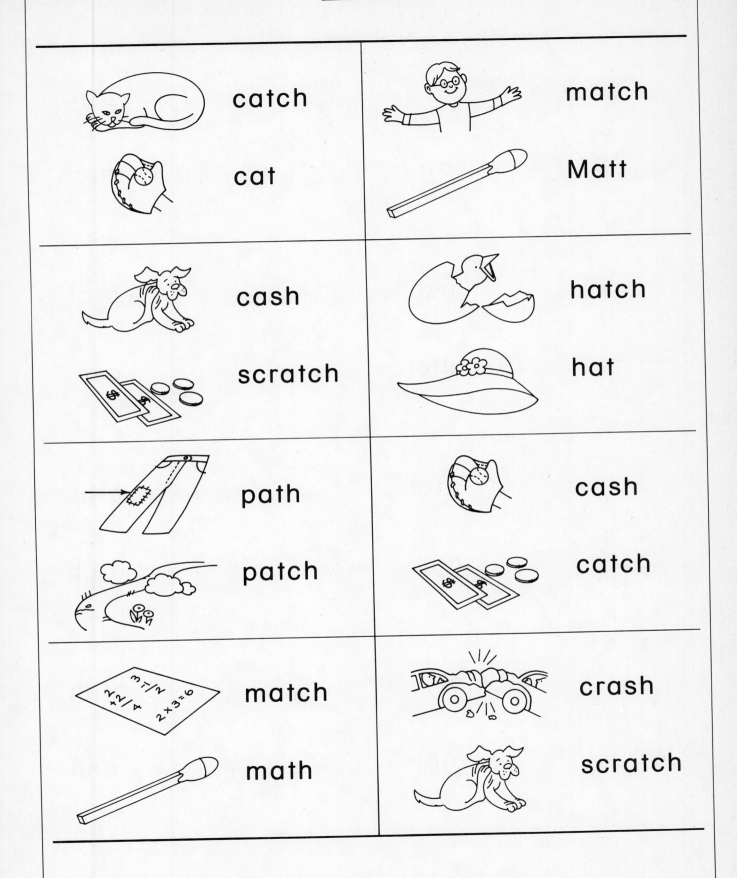

catch

cat

match

Matt

cash

scratch

hatch

hat

path

patch

cash

catch

match

math

crash

scratch

___ tch

h ___

at

atch

p ___

ath

atch

m ___

ash

atch

c ___

atch

ash

h ___

atch

at

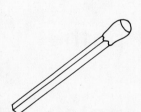
m ___

ath

atch

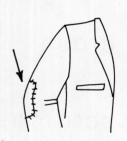
p ___

at

atch

w ___

atch

ash

1. Jeff is going to run to c_____ up to his pals.
   at   atch

2. Sid put on socks that did not m_____.
   at   atch

3. Trish will p_____ the ball to me.
   inch   itch

4. Max is pushing the sw_____ himself.
   ing   inch

5. Val is walking to the pond to w_____ me swim.
   atch   ash

6. Ann will trim the cr_____ off the bun.
   utch   ust

7. Bess fell into the shrub and got a scr_____.
   am   atch

8. Chad put a p_____ on the rip in his pants.
   at   atch

___etch ___itch ___utch

	itch
	_s_ _k_ etch
___ ___ ___etch	___ ___ itch
___ ___utch	___ itch

ditch	dish	Dutch	ditch	batch	ditch
pitch	pitch	pinch	prick	patch	pitch
hitch	hatch	hitch	hutch	hitch	ditch
stitch	stitch	sketch	snatch	stitch	stash
fetch	hutch	fish	fetch	hatch	fetch
hutch	hitch	hutch	hunch	hutch	hatch

cr	str	sw	p

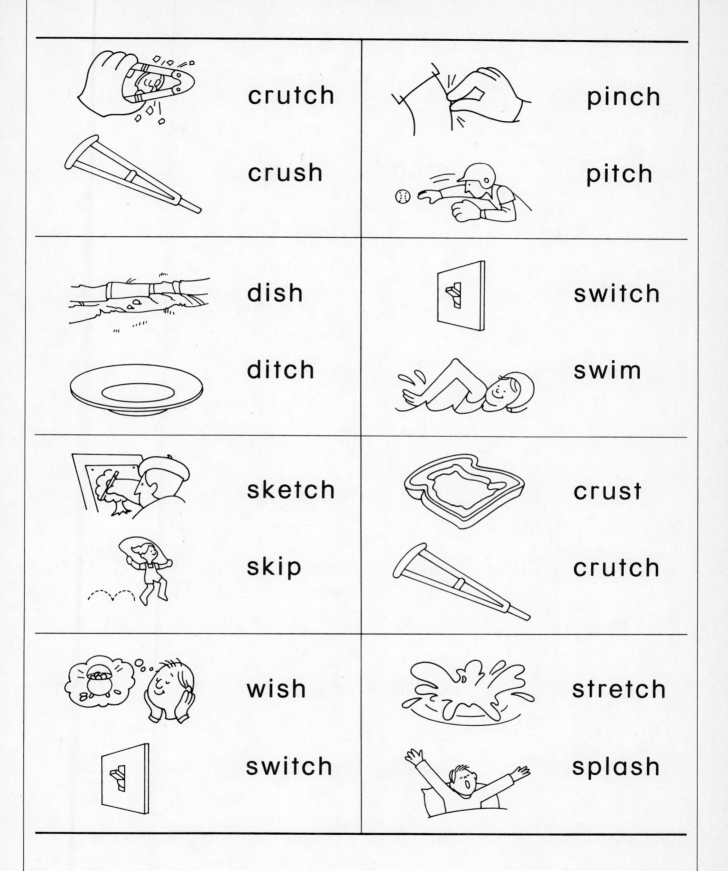

crutch

crush

pinch

pitch

dish

ditch

switch

swim

sketch

skip

crust

crutch

wish

switch

stretch

splash

___tch

f ___
ell
etch

sw ___
ish
itch

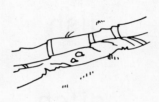

i ___
t
tch

d ___
itch
ish

d ___
itch
ish

p ___
it
itch

cr ___
utch
ush

w ___
itch
ish

___ tch

1. She will dress up as a w_____ in the skit.
   itch   ish

2. Bess will st_____ up the rip in the slacks.
   ick   itch

3. Peg is helping me cr_____ the big box.
   ush   utch

4. The dog is running to f_____ the stick.
   etch   ell

5. Liz will push the p_____ to the back of a shelf.
   atch   ans

6. We quit digging the d_____ to get a snack.
   ish   itch

7. Ask Kim to sw_____ on the TV set.
   ish   itch

8. She held up the hem of the dress with p_____.
   itch   ins

 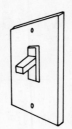

scratch

switch

branch

fetch

 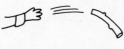 

lunch

bench

 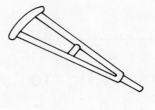

crutch

punch

 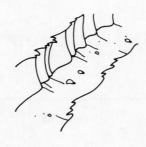

stretch

ditch

pinch

pitch

batch

bench

itch

inch

munch

match

latch

lunch

crutch

crunch

punch

patch

ditch

bunch

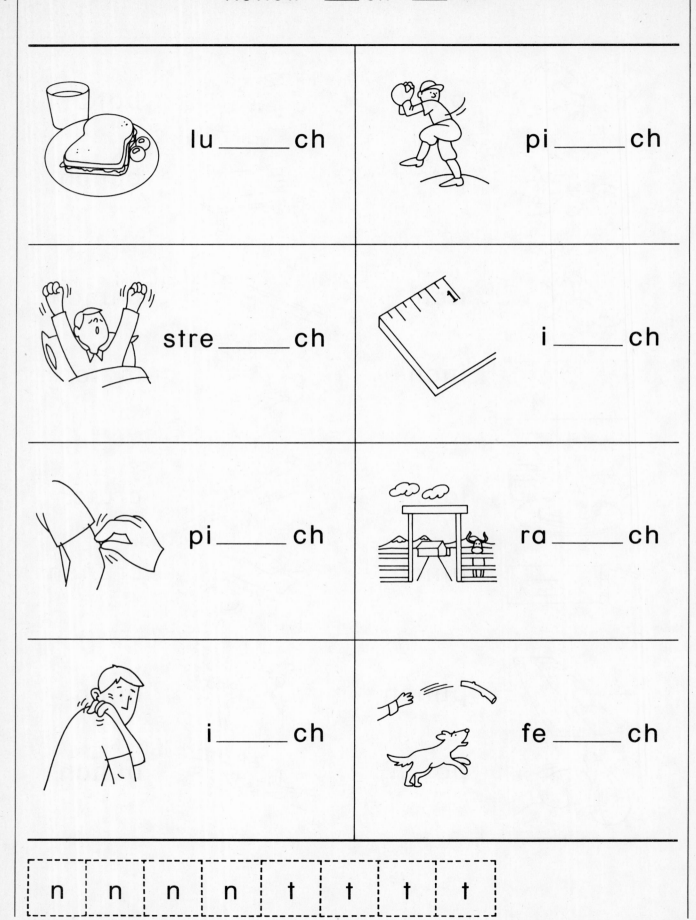

lu _____ ch

pi _____ ch

stre _____ ch

i _____ ch

pi _____ ch

ra _____ ch

i _____ ch

fe _____ ch

| n | n | n | n | t | t | t | t |

1. We put a _____ on the rip in the tent.
   patch punch

2. Tell Tom to flip on the _____.
   scrunch switch

3. Mitch can drink a malt with his _____.
   latch lunch

4. She is picking a _____ of mums.
   bunch batch

5. Jack had to rush to get to his _____ class.
   French fetch

6. Dad is pitching the ball. Ed will _____ it.
   catch crunch

7. The dog is scratching an _____ on its back.
   inch itch

8. The dog is running to _____ the ball.
   French fetch

w a   ___asp   ___amp   ___imp   ___ump

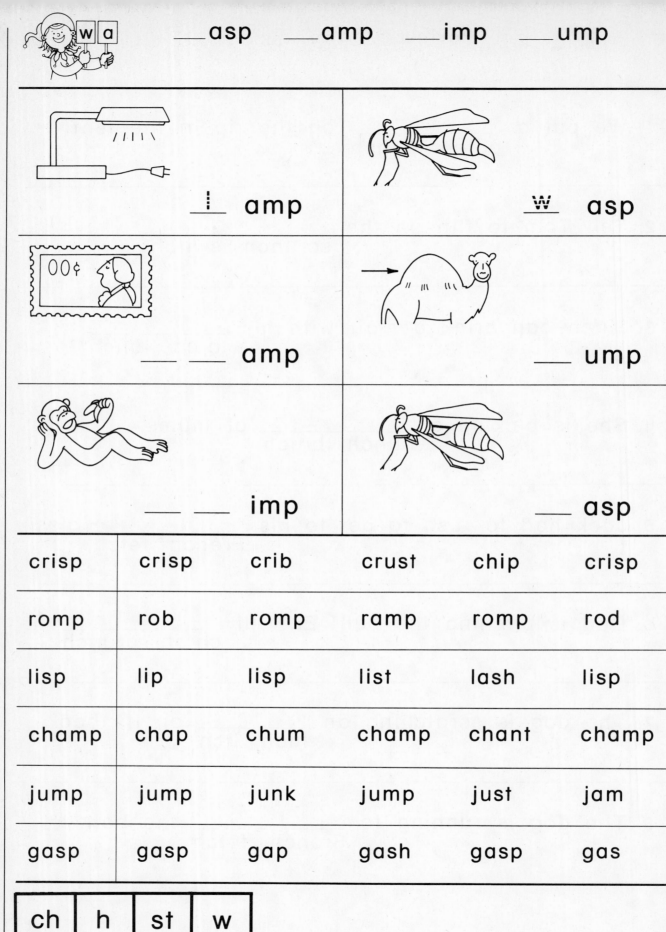

<u>l</u> amp

<u>w</u> asp

___ ___ amp

___ ump

___ ___ imp

___ asp

crisp	crisp	crib	crust	chip	crisp
romp	rob	romp	ramp	romp	rod
lisp	lip	lisp	list	lash	lisp
champ	chap	chum	champ	chant	champ
jump	jump	junk	jump	just	jam
gasp	gasp	gap	gash	gasp	gas

| ch | h | st | w |

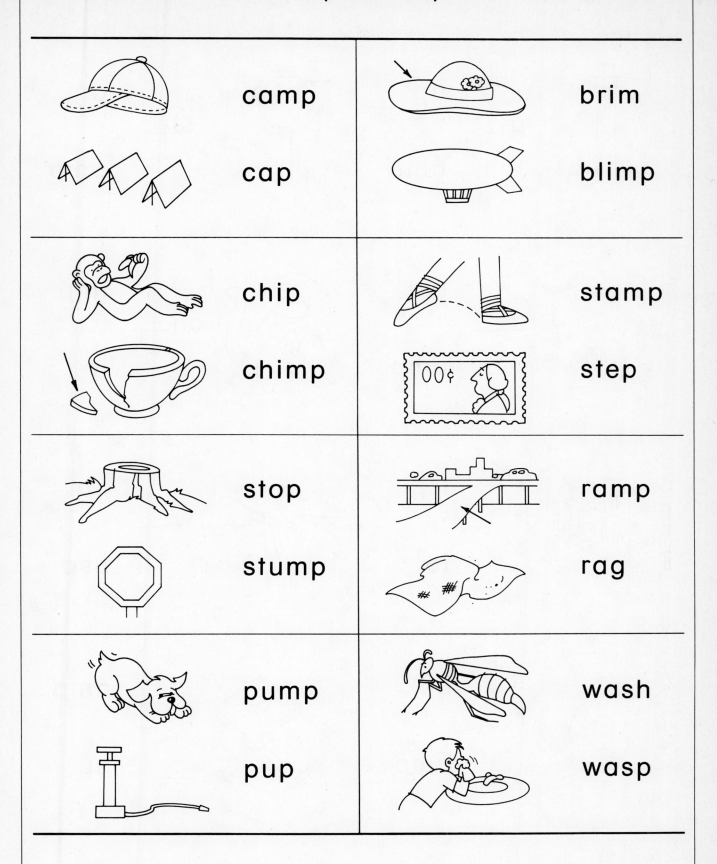

camp

cap

brim

blimp

chip

chimp

stamp

step

stop

stump

ramp

rag

pump

pup

wash

wasp

___ sp   ___ mp

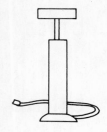

p ___

up

ump

st ___

op

omp

d ___

ust

ump

ch ___

imp

ip

cr ___

isp

ib

w ___

ag

asp

r ___

ock

omp

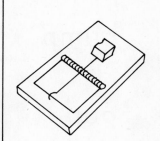

tr ___

amp

ap

 la ____ p

 ju ____ p

 chi ____ p

 hum ____

 ram ____

 wa ____ p

 bli ____ p

 stu ____ p

| m | m | m | m | m | p | p | s |

___ sp   ___ mp

1. The kids went to c_____.
   ap amp

2. The w_____ has a nest on the branch.
   asp ash

3. The cat can j_____ up on the shelf.
   ump ust

4. The ch_____ is swinging from the ring.
   imp ip

5. Mom had ham on a cr_____ bun.
   imp isp

6. He is scrubbing his hands at the p_____.
   ump up

7. Do not st_____ on the grass.
   ock omp

8. Jan will st_____ a lot of junk in the bag.
   uff ump

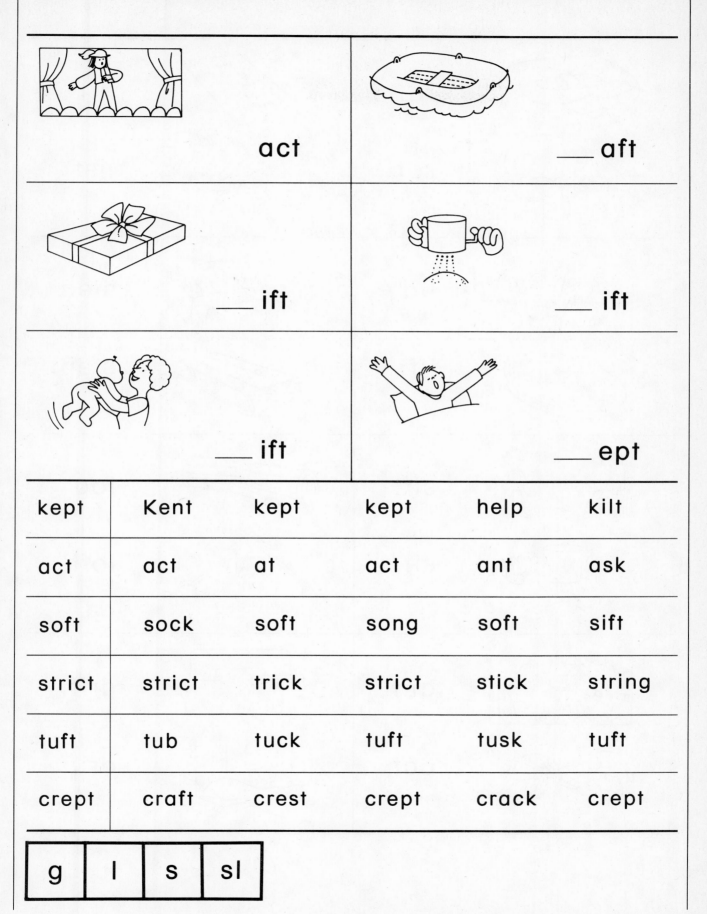

act

___ aft

___ ift

___ ift

___ ift

___ ept

kept	Kent	kept	kept	help	kilt
act	act	at	act	ant	ask
soft	sock	soft	song	soft	sift
strict	strict	trick	strict	stick	string
tuft	tub	tuck	tuft	tusk	tuft
crept	craft	crest	crept	crack	crept

g	l	s	sl

___ pt   ___ ft   ___ ct

	raft		lift
	rat		list
	lid		sled
	lift		slept
	sift		log
	sit		loft
	ant		drift
	act		drip

tr ___

act

ash

w ___

eb

ept

sw ___

ell

ept

r ___

aft

at

sh ___

ip

ift

s ___

ill

ift

sl ___

ept

ed

p ___

at

act

___pt ___ft ___ct

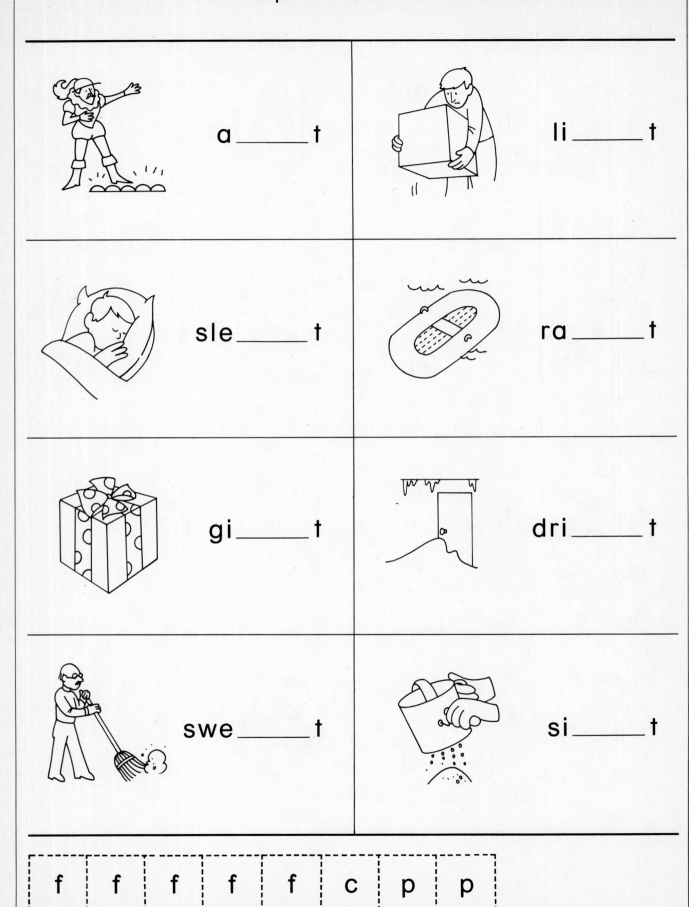

a ___ ___ t

li ___ ___ t

sle ___ ___ t

ra ___ ___ t

gi ___ ___ t

dri ___ ___ t

swe ___ ___ t

si ___ ___ t

| f | f | f | f | f | c | p | p |

1. The small cat felt s_____.
   ong oft

2. Cloth will stretch and get l_____ if you pull it.
   ong oft

3. Mom put a patch on the l_____ leg of the pants.
   eft ed

4. The twig will dr_____ on the pond.
   ip ift

5. The man can l_____ the log off the stack.
   ift ist

6. He will put his small sh_____ in the bathtub.
   ip ift

7. We will _____ in a skit in front of the class.
   an act

8. P_____ had a lunch of shrimp and crisp rolls.
   act am

a
drinks
She
malt

1. _____ _____ _____ _____ .

He
gift
a
sends

2. _____ _____ _____ _____ .

jumping
is
She
up

3. _____ _____ _____ _____ .

a
shrub
plants
He

4. _____ _____ _____ _____ .

1. Can you print with chalk?   yes   no

2. Can a switch go on and off?   yes   no

3. Can you plant a scratch?   yes   no

4. Can a skunk stink?   yes   no

5. Can you bend and stretch?   yes   no

6. Can you get a checkup from a bank? yes   no

7. Will string melt when it is hot?   yes   no

8. Can you jump into a pond and splash? yes   no

9. Is a Ping-Pong ball soft?   yes   no

10. Is jam crisp?   yes   no

Things you can put on: (7)

belt	trunk	ring	dress
swing	pants	twig	slacks
vest	hot	socks	shelf

Things that can walk: (6)

skunk	crutch	camp	king
plant	quilt	ant	hand
elk	man	stilts	chimp

Things you can do: (8)

think	melt	squint	act
splash	stretch	wash	wilt
gift	help	lamp	plant

Things you can get into: (7)

tent	bench	bunk	pond
gift	bathtub	lamp	truck
shelf	cab	bed	wind

Things you can pick up: (9)

ring	watch	milk	chalk
sand	salt	ranch	malt
wind	ant	lunchbox	pond

1. To mend is to _____ .
   shrink stitch squash

2. A bench is to _____ on.
   walk stand sit

3. To yank is to _____ .
   pull push yell

4. To shrink is to get _____ .
   big small long

5. A crutch is to help you _____ .
   wash jump walk

6. To scrub is to _____ .
   wash watch spring

7. To sprint is to _____ fast.
   talk run jump

8. To chat is to _____ .
   talk sing act

1. It has fish in it.
   It has sand and plants in it.
   You can help lift it.

   It is a fish _____ .

2. It has 4 legs.
   It is long.
   You can sit and rest on it.

   It is a _____ .

3. It can hang from a branch.
   You can sit on it.
   A push can help you go up.

   It is a _____ .

4. It is on the desk.
   It has a switch.
   It can go on and off.

   It is a _____ .

5. It is a bug with wings.
   It has a nest.
   It can sting you.

   It is a _____ .

bench	lamp	tank	chalk	swing
wasp	pond	dog	wash	nest